A Half-Baked Fruitcake of Nuts and Nonsense

Silly stuff for kids of all ages

Poems and illustrations
John Jenkins

© John Jenkins 2021 (text & images)

This book is copyright. Apart from any fair dealing for the purposes of study and research, criticism, review or as otherwise permitted under the Copyright Act, no part may be reproduced by any process without written permission. Inquiries should be made to the publisher.

First published in 2021
Published by Busybird Publishing
www.busybird.com.au

ISBN: 978-1-922465-65-8
A catalogue record for this book is available from the National Library Australia.

Cover design: John Jenkins
Text design: Busybird Publishing

Contents

The Wilderong	4
Rainbow Riding	6
Shaun the Leprechaun	7
Witches Have Hitches	8
Little Figures Dancing	9
The Long-Nosed Smelter	10
My Name is Alphonse	12
Hey, My Name is Alphonse Too!	13
Come Fry With Me	14
The Weasel and the Skink	15
Bubbles the Clever Dolphin	16
Breaking Surface!	17
Chef Cooker-burra	18
Cooking the Numbers	19
The Jolly Joker	20
The Hen on My Cup	21
Go Anna!	22
Tales of a Dragon's Tails	23
Around the Peppercorn Tree	24
Miranda's Chooky Squawkestra	25
Double Header	26
Busy Mrs. Mouse	27
Pedro the Pencil Mouse	28
According to Accordionists	29
'Ding! Ding!	30
Archie the Alien	31
Percy the Giraffe	32

Art Lover Mike	33
When Burble Became 'elbruB'	34
Three Mugs and Three Bottles	35
Welcome to Piggly Park!	36
Little Pizov the Caravan Sets Out	37
The Happy Neighborhood	38
Cruising Clyde, the Cool Car with Wings	39
Hermione's Comb	40
Gorilla on a Pillar	41
The Big, Crazy, Fish-Wheel Ride	42
Terry and Goldie	43
Mr. Frog to Mr. Mozzie	44
Toady and Hopper at the Pool	45
Egbert's Grand Egg Burst	46
The Unruffled Flower Bed	47
That Ancient Greek Geek	48
Wayne, the Not-So-Dumb Ox	49
The Little Humming Cup Boat	50
Three See-Saw Ladies	51
Two Toucans	52
The Little Wheel Horse With the Curly-Whirly Tail	53
Two Bright Drinks	54
When Mr. Blockhead Spins	55
Louis's 'Light-bulb Moment'	56
Mr. Treble Clef	57
Marcel the Poodle	58
Party Piece	60
The Space Clown, Mr. Pocket Rocket	61
Noisy Cicadas	62
The Rubber Band	63

The Piano in the Shed	64
Hush, Hush, a Lullaby	65
Moon Flakes	66
The Vase From Mars	67
Billy the Goat	68
On Monkey Island	69
Juniper Jim	70
Leo's Annual Health Check	71
Sir Laugh-a-lot	72
Steady Edward the Spinning Top	74
Dashing Dan Steps Out	75
Catpencil Lid	76
Harry, the Half-Baked Gingerbread Man	78
Mr. Caterpillar Aims High	79
The House on Two Legs	80
Fernley, the Little Blast Furnace	82
Acknowledgements:	85
Note on the Author/Illustrator:	87
Thank you:	87

The Wilderong

1. The Wilderong is the most amazing beast
   That you could ever see
   As it streaks above the stratosphere
   On genuflecting knee.

2. From trees of cork to trees of oak
   It can swing from night to noon,
   Then crinkles up its ghastly toes
   And plays a snide bassoon.

3. On a snide bassoon with big blue stars
   It blurts a doleful wail,
   To sound around the lost lagoons
   And wake the sleepy snail.

4. A tune that would make a catfish shrink
   Or a Marmaduke think twice –
   A tune to swoon to, a tune to croon to,
   A tune to break the ice.

5. Then after the last note has died
   On its ghastly way it goes,
   But if you ask me where or why
   I must answer: NO ONE KNOWS.

Rainbow Riding

Riding around rainbows
Is so good to do,
Riding down rainbows
Stretching high in the sky
Where only eagles and aeroplanes fly.

        Past soft clouds in the sky
        I push off so high,
        I ride around and around
        In an old dressing gown,
        Then bounce back off the ground!

        Rainbow colors all dance,
        In big painted bands,
        Sliding down red and blue,
        While below I see ants,
        Sliding down, on the seat of my pants!

Shaun the Leprechaun

1. That funny Leprechaun
   Whose name was Shaun,
   Riding on a scooter
   With its big brass hooter.

   2. To be sure to be sure
      Shaun grinned from his core,
      With his umbrella held high
      As gold fell from the sky.

      3. "I'm from the Emerald Isle
         Where rainbows all smile
         After pots of gold rain
         Fall again and again.

         4. "On my scooter I hop
            When that sunny gold drops,
            Then scoop up the lot
            Into big rainbow pots!"

Witches Have Hitches

Witches have hitches
    In their funny black britches
And bits of straw from the end of their brooms
    And they often get itches
And backstroke and fitses
    From flying too close to the moon.

Little Figures Dancing

Little figures dancing
Up and down they go,
Dancing in the sunshine
And putting on a show.

Little figures laughing,
Hopping into town,
Little figures singing,
Prancing up and down.

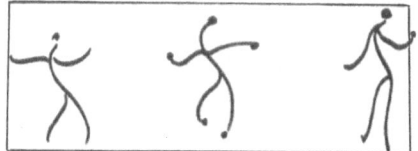

    Little figures playing
    On their violins,
    As lovely notes of music
    Are bowed up from their strings.

Little figures strutting,
Whirling with neat feet,
Clapping hands and smiling
At everyone they meet.

    Because they know that dancing
    And hopping down the street
    Is so much fun to do
    And makes each day complete!

The Long-Nosed Smelter

We're going for a ride on the Smelter's nose
We're taking a cabbage and a fresh change of clothes.
It will be such fun, you should come too,
There'll be so much to see and so much to do.
Uncle Horace is coming, and also his brother,
Wild Whistling Willie, and so many others –
A goat that wears glasses, three fish that all sneeze,
Two terrible pancakes and the elephant's fleas.
Come with us for a ride on the Smelter,
For a ride on the side of his nose, oh do!
It wouldn't be fun if we went by ourselves,
It wouldn't be fun if you didn't come too.

But you're saying you will? I just knew you would,
For rambling and scrambling on the nose of a Smelter
As he rumbles and stumbles all over the woods,
Puts a shine on your belly, a sprat in your ear,
A crease in your toes and makes you look good.
But where can we place you – his nose is so packed?
Place you or race you, it's space that is lacked.
We'll put you in front on a deck chair of red,
On a high horse-hair hammock or a fine feather bed,
As he swings through the trees or crawls on his knees,
You can go climbing all over his head.

My Name is Alphonse

My name is Alphonse
And I walk on stilts.
I sway, then I play
If one bends or tilts.

My tail asks a question
And I wear a big hat.
I do this all day,
That's why I'm not fat.

As the four winds blow,
With the sun in my eye,
I just laugh and sing,
Walking high in the sky!

Hey, My Name is Alphonse Too!

My name is Alphonse too,
And I also walk on stilts.
I like to take the air up here
And don't mind if one stilt tilts.

I'm not afraid of falling
Because I have wings to fly.
And did I also mention
That I wear a nice bow tie?

See Alphonse One and Two
Go stepping out together,
Showing off their silly tricks
And never mind the weather!

Come Fry With Me

Come fry with me,
Come fry, come fry away!
Up in the sky so blue,
Let's fry some clouds today.

Come fry, come fry away
Let's try some rainbow stew
Up in the morning dew.
We'll fry five pancakes too!

The Weasel and the Skink

The weasel and the skink
Play card games every day,
But when weasel has to sneeze
The skink must slink away,

To make hot lemon juice
For the weasel on a tray,
So both can stay sneeze-less
And play on, come what may!

Bubbles the Clever Dolphin

Bubbles the clever Dolphin
Always likes to draw graphs.
She calls out "Whoopie-doo!"
And is very good at maths.

She draws graphs of shellfish
And maps of coast and land.
She maps out coral reefs
And draws pictures in the sand.

When all her graphs are finished
She calls out "Woopie-doo!"
Then has a cup of tea
And a sardine sand-wich too!

Breaking Surface!

When Mr. Seal breaks surface
He blows a giant bubble,
He yodels to some codfish
But always stays out of trouble!

He dives and he somersaults,
Swimming at the double,
And he plays with big pink prawns
But always stays out of trouble!

He barks at breaking waves
And juggles minnows in a puddle.
He is our a 'seal of approval'
Because he stays out of trouble!

Chef Cooker-burra

1. Cooker-burra the chef
   Was cooking his tea.
   He invited a possum
   And an emu and me.

2. He cooked gum-nut soup
   And paper-bark stew,
   He roasted big pumpkins
   And a turnip or two.

3. He cooked nice pancakes
   With strawberry cream
   So his happy cuisine
   Tasted like a sweet dream.

4. He invited a wombat
   And a big bumble bee,
   Then set up his table
   Way up high in a tree.

5. He chuckled and said,
   "Please come over for tea.
   Just bring your big tummy,
   And then climb up with me!"

Cooking the Numbers

This Electric Waffle Iron
He cooked numbers, never food.
But customers he cooked for
Thought this was pretty rude.

"We would rather have waffles
Or a nice flapjack or two,
Please, no more arithmetic,
Even a slice of toast will do!"

So the waffle iron smiled
And stopped cooking sums,
But whipped up tempting treats
Which they tucked into their tums!

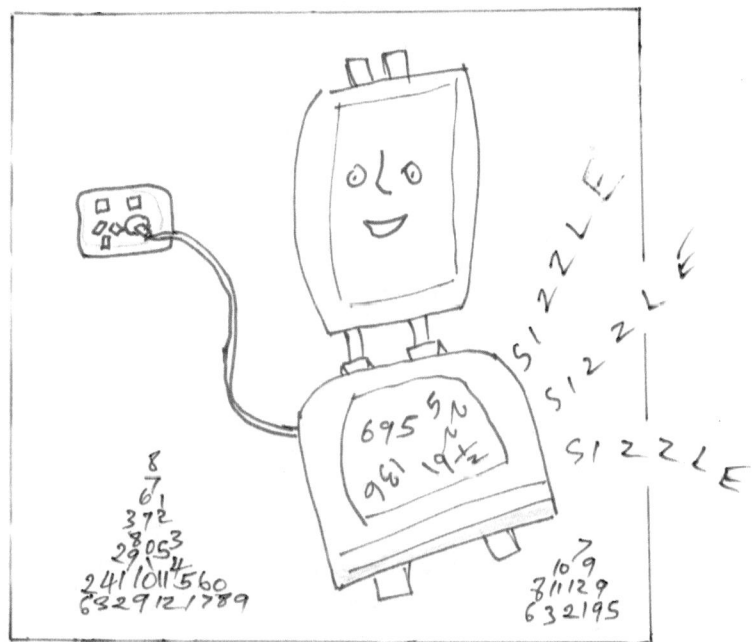

The Jolly Joker

The Jolly Joker was a card
Always leaping in the air,
He just laughed up both his sleeves
And spread sunshine everywhere!

        He would never bet real money
        When playing snap or poker,
        But threw his cards into the clouds,
        That's why he was a Joker!

The Hen on My Cup

They call me 'chook picture',
But I'm really a hen.
I was drawn onto my cup
With a brush and a pen.

If you pick up this cup,
Then please look at me.
And I will wink back at you
Just as you sip your tea!

Go Anna!

Anna is a goanna
With a very pleasant manner,
Who gathers flowers everywhere
And throws them in the air.

      She plucks buttercups too
      And roses glazed with dew,
      Then the petals that she throws
      Float down around her nose!

Tales of a Dragon's Tails

"No bragging, I'm a smart dragon!
And I've three heads and tails.
I've just told one, and so
I've got two more 'tales' to go.

      "My next one is the shortest,
      I use for opening cans
      And slapping flies as well…
      Which leaves one tale left to tell.

"My third tail is the longest
But today I'll tell it fast.
All day it's wound up tight,
Then I sleep on it at night!

      "By the way, I like chilies
      And I eat them all the time.
      They poke my smoke much higher up
      When my three tongues all catch fire!"

Around the Peppercorn Tree

1. Around the peppercorn tree,
   To see what I've just seen
   Is where I've already been
   As my tail chases me…!

   2. Yes, off again it slips!
      As I stop a while to see
      If it still follows me…
      Then round the tree it whips!

3. So it's off I leap again
   As it runs away so fast!
   I'll try to catch my tail at last,
   But who knows where or when?

Miranda's Chooky Squawkestra

A chooky choir is called a 'squawkestra'
As they sing high up on a perch.
First, they tune their pretty beaks
Going cluck-cluck-cluck for all they're worth!

"One two, now clucky-cluck girls,"
Is egg-zackly how notes loop and swoop.
They all sing so im-peck-ably
Perched inside their chicken coop.

They all squawk and hold their beaks up high,
As Miranda swings her big baton
And helps them cluck in perfect time
For their happy chooky sing-along!

Double Header

Why are two heads
Better than one?
Buying new hats
Is twice the fun.

Busy Mrs. Mouse

Mrs. Mouse was always busy,
And she wore a lot of bling,
She liked things neat and tidy,
And as she swept she'd sing.

But one Sunday she got lucky
And swept up a diamond ring.
Now she can pay her cousin
To sweep up everything!

Pedro the Pencil Mouse

Pedro the pencil mouse
Flew all the way from Spain,
He knew where to draw the line
Or rub it out again.

He took drawing lessons
From a most artistic snail.
He drew his own moustache
Then Pedro drew his tail.

He sharpened up his act
In fine pencil lines so thin.
Then yelled "hello" to all his fans
Just to draw them in!

According to Accordionists

Accordionists say
Stay close to each table,
And play a good tune
As best as you're able.

    But if no guest turns up
    To partake of your fare,
    You can play quite nicely
    To a big empty chair.

        And if doggie joins in,
        With loud howls from the floor,
        Simply toss him a bone
        Then demand an encore!

'Ding! Ding!

Now! Two fighters slip into the ring!
First it's 'Spud', then we see,
As the starting bell dings,
Tall 'Thud', the boxing zucchini!

With their gloves held up high
They skip out and attack.
They both leap and they fly
Round the ring and then back.

'Thud' can throw a quick right,
As he's so often boasted,
And when he throws one tonight
'Spud' is peeled, baked and roasted!

Archie the Alien

Archie the Alien
With his head in the stars
Took a long holiday
To Venus and Mars.

With his head in the clouds
He zoomed right down to Earth
And made many new friends
In Melbourne and Perth.

He said, "Hi you Earthlings!"
Stepping out on pink feet.
Then Archie had lunch
And tried new things to eat,

Like saucers of ice-cream
And burnt lemon pud.
Then choc-coated door knobs
Which tasted so good.

He looked up from his spoons
And said, "Now time to fly!"
Then filled his big saucer
And flew up to the sky.

Percy the Giraffe

1. Percy the giraffe,
   Was nick-named 'Stretch'
   'Cause there was nothing too high
   That he couldn't fetch!

2. But Percy often coughed
   If he grinned or he laughed,
   So he chewed lots of leaves
   Did that happy giraffe.

3. He munched lolly leaves,
   Fresh green and dark brown.
   Percy smiled as they slipped
   All that long, loooong way down!

4. First he swallowed one
   Then chewed twenty more
   Because his neck didn't tickle
   And was no looooooonger sore!

Art Lover Mike

1. For keen art lover Mike
   A gallery was like
   A great big artwork zoo.
   At exhibitions in town
   Mike would dance all around
   As his love of art grew.

2. One day Mike said, "Wait on!"
   And he tied on an apron.
   Now Mike knew what to do!
   It was such a huge blast
   To fashion sculptures at last
   Plus a statue or two!

When Burble Became 'elbruB'

When Burble drove backwards
He rattled down the hill.
He went elbruB right down,
And felt such a dill.

      Though driving in reverse
      Wasn't just standing still,
      To Burble back up faster
      Was much more of a thrill!

Three Mugs and Three Bottles

Three mugs and three bottles
All went out to town.
Three mugs and three bottles
Hopped round and around.

Three mugs and three bottles
Danced round in a ring.
Three mugs and three bottles
All had quite a fling.

3. Three mugs and three bottles
   Said, "What do you think?"
   Three mugs and three bottles
   Poured drink after drink

4. Three mugs and three bottles
   Drank more and more!
   They were really 'mugs' now,
   All 'smashed' on the floor!

Welcome to Piggly Park!

We've been invited to Piggly Park
To be met by Lord Grunt at the gate,
We're having an afternoon mud bath with him,
So bring soap and do not be late!

At Piggly Park you are welcome to dine
At a nice picnic spot by the lake.
Lord Grunt eats a bucket or two of stew
And mixes his meals with a rake.

Lord Grunt likes turnips and pink fizzy gin
And he wears a bow tie and top hat.
Admire his moustache and big double chin,
But please don't tell him he's fat!

Little Pizov the Caravan Sets Out

Little Pizov the cute caravan
Hitched himself to a car.
He went to see Oz-stray-ya,
Then off he rolled, "Tat-tah!"

Down a long and bumpy road
That was very hard to steer,
Pizov crossed a river bank
And camped there for a year.

Then further on he rolled,
Down far valleys short and long,
Then climbed a winding trail
While singing this bright song:

"I've reached the top of Two-Tree Hill,
To enjoy the evening view,
I'll just unhitch myself here now
Then do what Pizov's do!"

The Happy Neighborhood

This neighborhood is so merry
Where the sun shines down all day.
The houses wear their happy hats
As people work and play.

The people gossip and they dance
And no one breathes a sigh.
All singing songs and then they prance
While clouds are drifting by.

It's such a happy neighborhood
With neat gardens in a row
And when the rain falls from the clouds
It makes those gardens grow!

Cruising Clyde, the Cool Car with Wings

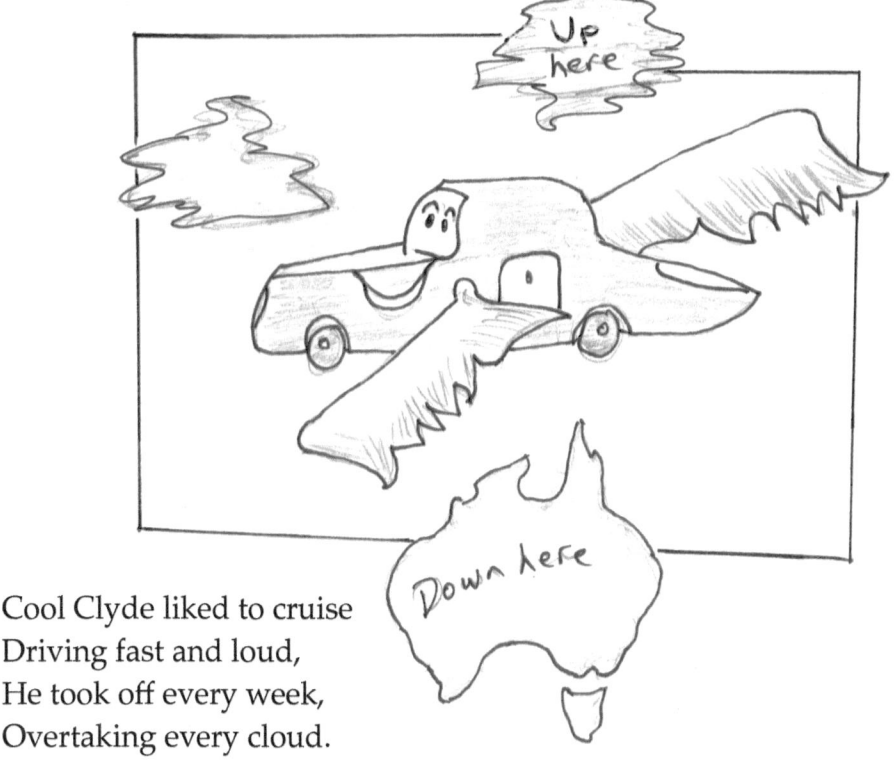

Cool Clyde liked to cruise
Driving fast and loud,
He took off every week,
Overtaking every cloud.

    Clyde liked to stretch his wings
    By driving way up there,
    Like any aviator
    Clyde sped into the air.

Clyde flew past Darwin
Then he took a little nap
Dashing over Melbourne
And almost off the map.

    That cool car called Clyde
    Doesn't have a care,
    On his big sky highway
    He goes cruising everywhere!

Hermione's Comb

Hermione had a lovely comb,
As nice as a comb could be.
She combed out her tail feathers
And the leaves of every tree.

                    She combed the fields for seeds
                    And did hairdos for a fee!
                    She could even jump out of this page
                    And start combing you and me!

Gorilla on a Pillar

George the gorilla
Climbed to the top of a pillar
And called Lovey Dovey to play.
She tossed him bananas
Did that sweet birdie charmer
And George caught ten every day.

George loved it up there
Sitting high in the air,
He really thought it was grand
As Lovey Dovey flew by
Tossing bananas so high
And then watched them land in his hand!

The Big, Crazy, Fish-Wheel Ride

The big, crazy fish-wheel ride
Is a high Ferris wheel in the park.
It makes fish feel fizzy and very dizzy,
As they take turns watching for sharks.

They ride every day after 'school' here,
But there's not a drop of water up there.
Still, they don't have to swim very far,
But just spin on their fins through the air!

Terry and Goldie

When entertainer Terry
Goes crack with his big whip,
Little Goldie leaps so high
In a slippery flip!

    Water flies up in the air
    Beneath their circus tent
    And the crowds all stare and point
    To see where Goldie went!

        Goldie is a big splash hit
        And leaps her daring loop,
        Flying up into the air
        Then straight through Terry's hoop!

Mr. Frog to Mr. Mozzie

"Fly over to my place,"
Said fat Mr. Frog,
"It's so soft and green,
Not like some old log.

"Come sit with me
On my big shiny leaf,
Where cool water sparkles
All day underneath.

"Buzz over for lunch
And I'll shout croak-croak!'
You can perch on my pad
And tell me your jokes!

"Yes, Mr. Mozzie,
Just fly over, please do,
And when I say 'Snap!'
Then lunch is on you!"

Toady and Hopper at the Pool

1. Toady and Hopper
   Were two little frogs
   Who always felt bored
   Just sitting on logs.

2. "I'd much rather jump,"
   Fat Toady said,
   "In a big tin bucket
   And swim there instead!"

3. Hopper cried, "Me first!"
   Then off they both dashed
   To find a tin bucket,
   And into it splashed.

4. Toady croaked loudly,
   "Hey, watch me swim!"
   And did a belly whack,
   Just as Hopper jumped in!

Egbert's Grand Egg Burst

There once was a chicken called Egbert
Who went tat-tap-tap on his shell,
Then poked up through his egg-lid
As his old world splintered and fell.

There was no match for this hatchling
Now a new world he could see,
As Egbert smiled and he tweeted,
"Hey, it feels so good to be me!"

The Unruffled Flower Bed

This bed is full of flowers
Growing from end to end,
As rugs of clover glisten
And roses shimmer and bend.

    There are silky sheets of ferns
    Amidst blossoms blue and red
    And pillows of soft petals
    To tuck under sleepy heads.

You can laze around all day
As honey bees take flight,
Then snuggle under your doona
As frogs hop round all night!

That Ancient Greek Geek

A Greek geek called Democritus
Was born in ancient Thrace,
Who first guessed that tiny atoms
Filled up all matter's space.

Yes, those atoms that he sat on,
Though so small and hard to see,
They made up all of matter
Including you and me.

He now sits high on a pillar
That still bears his famous name,
Where that smart atom guesser
Enjoys a lasting fame.

Wayne, the Not-So-Dumb Ox

Wayne the ox was quite a dunce.
He always got things wrong
All the time, not just once.
If what he tried didn't work,
He did the same thing again.
It almost drove Wayne berserk!

But Wayne knew why plants grew
When he worked out just how
They liked sun and rain too!
Wayne then grew smart in a blink!
When he sees the world now
He just says: Wayne, stop and think!

The Little Humming Cup Boat

This little humming cup boat
Floats out far to sea,
Where she hums all afternoon
Then croons to you and me:

> "I'm just a humming cup boat
> And I sing with joyful pride,
> Oh come along with me
> And we'll sail out with the tide!

> "Let's cross the oceans blue
> And steam into the sun!
> And as I splash and go toot-toot
> You can also hum along!"

Three See-Saw Ladies

I saw three see-saw ladies
Who jump and leap and hop,
Kicking up their heels
As their balloons pop.

Each one wears a pretty dress
With flowers in her hat.
Holding their balloons,
They sway all day like that.

    Balloons keep them steady,
    So they don't miss or mess.
    Swaying up and down,
    They certainly impress!

Two Toucans

Big Beak was a toucan
And Feathers was one too.
They baked new loaves of bread
As toucans often do.

Feathers pecked up one piece
But Big Beak wanted two.
They pecked up every tasty crumb,
Then off both toucans flew!

(Now all birds like to take a peck
So my story must be true!
If any cook can bake fresh bread,
Then so can toucans too!)

The Little Wheel Horse With the Curly-Whirly Tail

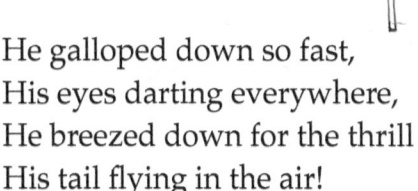

The little wheel horse
With the curly-whirly tail
Loved to roll down quickly,
To the bottom of his rail!

He galloped down so fast,
His eyes darting everywhere,
He breezed down for the thrill
His tail flying in the air!

On all his rapid runs
At the start of each new day,
He'd whinny down so easily
Before he munched some hay!

Two Bright Drinks

The light-bulb said:
"Hey, you nice little drink!
Tell me, what do you see,
And what do you think?"

The little glass said:
"I see, near the sink,
A lovely big tumbler,
Who is smiling I think.
So let's clink our glasses,
And toss down a drink!"

The light-bulb said:
"Hey – what a nice thing to do!
Do you mind if I join you?
Because I'm thirsty too!"

When Mr. Blockhead Spins

When Mr. Blockhead spins
He spins in outer space.
He spins past stars and moons,
He spins at quite a pace.

He spins so fast he leaves at dawn
And comes back the previous night,
Because he spins so fast
Almost at the speed of light.

He is made of bits of fence posts
And he loves to spin and race.
He is made of wood and timber –
And with such a beaming face!

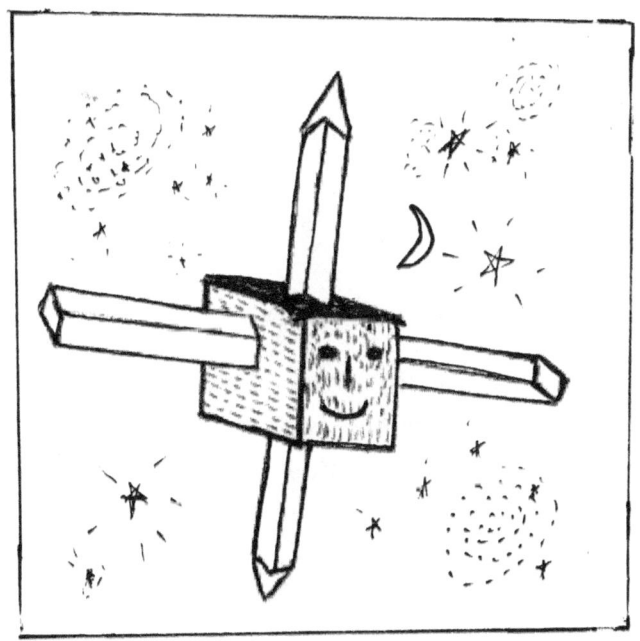

Louis's 'Light-bulb Moment'

Louis the light-bulb had an idea.
Louis's brain-wave was so simple and clear.
"Now my idea will stun everyone –
I'll just change myself! Then shine like the sun!"

Mr. Treble Clef

Mr. Treble Clef
Just turned up for the show
With a brand new tune to play
And his notes all in a row.

        Treble wore a tall top hat
        And nice red floppy tie,
        Then he smiled at each note
        As he hummed both low and high.

That Clef kept one eye
On all his notes there in a row.
He conducted them so quickly
While they walked high and low.

        Each footnote then stepped out
        Beating time with its new shoe!
        So just nodding his big head
        Was all Clef then had to do!

Marcel the Poodle

Marcel the poodle
Ate oodles of noodles
And *haute cuisine*
From his fork.

He wolfed down *croissants,*
Soufflé and *poulet*
And duos of *baguettes*
Served with pork.

"It's a mere *bagatelle*
To dine out so well,"
Said stylish Marcel
Looking great.

"A true *gourmet* like me
Has *éclairs* with tea
Plus a big pile of snails
On his plate.

"And I'm fond of *fondue*
Or a *gateau* or two
With a bowl of French fries
Till I'm sate."

With a glass in his paw
Marcel poured himself more
Bordeaux red and some fizzy champagne,
Then he sniffed and he licked AND HE ATE!

Party Piece

I love to go to parties
And spoil all the fun
By sitting in the custard tarts
And throwing buttered buns.

The Space Clown, Mr. Pocket Rocket

My name is Two Hats
Though I only have one.
It is balanced 'upstairs'
And flies off when I run.

And a miniature rocket
Is tucked into my pocket.
There it goes, *Whooooosh!*
Blasting off just for fun!

Noisy Cicadas

Two very loud cicadas
Are tap-dancing on a drum,
While their sleepy friend
Hardly says *thrum-thrumm*,
But folds his wings up slowly
While snoozing in the sun.

The Rubber Band

There was an electric duo
Who were both made of rubber.
They played guitar and bass
Making music with each-other.

The bass went *bump-bump*
And guitar went *twang-twang*.
They pulled out some new tunes
As people's ears went *bang*!

Their songs were bold and snappy
And playing quite elastic.
By stretching out their notes
They always sounded fantastic!

The Piano in the Shed

1. The piano in the shed
   Lived there all alone:
   "If I could make some music,
   I would really feel at home!"

2. So he floated up a note
   By pressing black or white,
   He played a few new chords
   Which all sounded just right

3. When he floated up more notes,
   It didn't take him long
   To invent some catchy tunes
   And compose a brand new song.

4. He tinkled on a high beam,
   And tonkled on a rafter,
   He played hard rock and classics
   And filled that shed with laughter!

Hush, Hush, a Lullaby

Oh hush, hush, a lullaby,
Child of quiet stars,
Lay down your sweet head,
Snuggle up in your bed,
Then drift away to Mars.

Say goodbye to this day
In your nice, cozy room.
You will soon be asleep
On clouds soft and deep,
As time fades away so soon.

The moon shines in the sky,
Like dreams so far away,
With all those sparkles falling
As the Milky Way is calling
For you to come and play.

See the shimmering sky,
Where galaxies all whirl.
Lay down your sweet head
In your soft space-ship bed
As your gentle dreams unfurl.

Moon Flakes

1. See the moon flakes falling
   And covering your town,
   Drifting in the darkness,
   See them falling down.

2. Gently they all glide
   On the chilly, soft night air,
   Shiny silver moon flakes
   Are falling everywhere.

3. More moon flakes drift down,
   So fragile and so rare,
   Falling on your shoulders
   And catching in your hair.

4. See the moon flakes falling,
   And when they fall your way
   Sprinkle them on buttered toast
   For your breakfast the next day!

The Vase From Mars

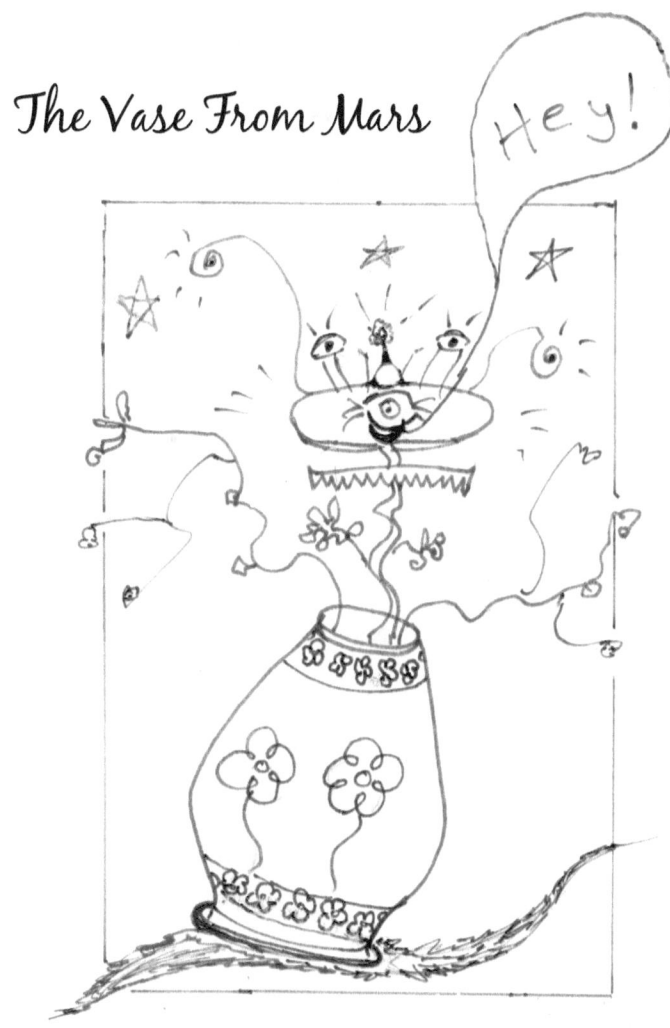

Hey you, I'm Mr. Ten Eyes!
And I'm the vase from Mars!
I can wave my tentacles about,
Wink and stare and scream and shout!

Hey, now I'm down here on Earth!
I've just landed in my saucer.
I'm from outer space, it's true –
And I've got ten eyes on you!

Billy the Goat

A singing goat will never gloat
When you put him up on stage.
A singing goat will clear his throat
And knows how to behave.

        This actor wore a funny horn
        Which one day just appeared,
        Then grew a stumpy tail half sawn
        And a little goatee beard.

His stage name was 'Mr. Gee',
Or plain Billy to his friends,
And when he acted up the goat
The applause would never end.

        After telling very silly jokes,
        About toucans baking bread
        He made his fans all laugh and cheer
        By standing on his head.

On Monkey Island

1. Monkey lived on an island,
   He lived there all alone,
   It was a tiny island
   But for monkey it was home.

2. In the middle of the island
   There grew a big palm tree,
   Where coconuts splashed down
   Every day into the sea.

3. Monkey put a note in one
   And he threw it in the drink.
   He wrote down, "Please visit soon!"
   And that floater didn't sink.

4. So if you find Monkey's message
   Get a boat and say hello:
   "Mr. Monkey, please hop aboard
   And I'll take you for a row!"

Juniper Jim

Juniper Jim
Is very thin
As well as very old.
And if it wasn't for
The length of his beard
He would catch his death of cold.

Leo's Annual Health Check

Leo the lion is so patient
Whenever his doctor sees him.
Leo holds his grinning head up high
And always tries to please him.

"His doctor says, "Please open wide,"
"Mr. Leo, just say '*Aaahh!*'
But lions always have to roar,
And so Leo he shouts '*Grrrhh!*'

Sir Laugh-a-lot

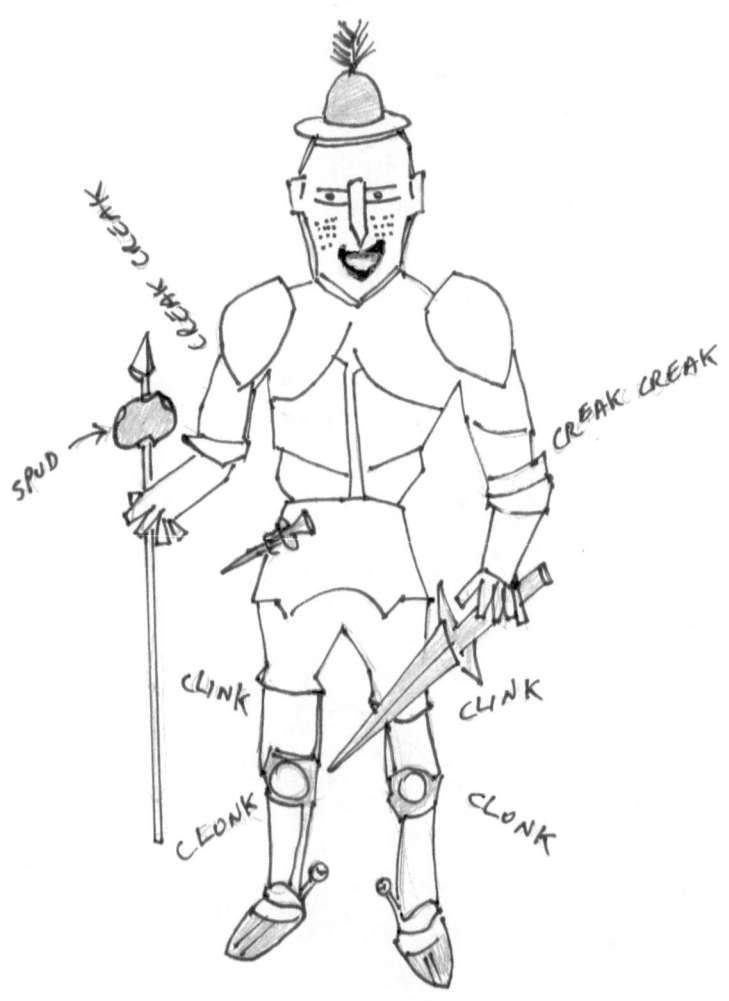

Sir Laugh-a-lot was a funny knight
Who always looked his best.
He never went out jousting,
He'd much rather snore and rest.

He wore panels of shiny armour
With hinges in the middle.
He sometimes wore a silly hat
And often played the fiddle.

He polished up his armor
Just because it looked so chic,
But when he forgot to oil it,
He would often clink and creak.

He kept a long spear handy
For hot-roasting spuds or beet,
Then poked them in his campfire
To have something nice to eat.

He wore his trusty armor,
He even wore it in his bed,
He put turnips in his helmet
Or boiled tea up there instead.

He wore his armor backwards
With all its hinges inside out.
That's why he always laughed a lot
As he clanked and clonked about.

Steady Edward the Spinning Top

Always whizzed round into town.
And he would never drop or stop,
With his big toe in the ground.

Eddy was not so skinny
Because Eddy loved to munch,
But stayed quite fast and steady
As he whirled around for lunch.

Lunch soon?

Dashing Dan Steps Out

Dan the Duck went for a waddle.
He put on his suit and favorite shoes!
"What a perfect day to go for a toddle!"
He met his good friend, Little Quack, out there,
Who thought Dan looked so debonair.

> Then Dan almost stepped in a puddle.
> As Little Quack splashed about in his lake.
> So Dashing Dan, he felt in a muddle,
> Because water was flying everywhere
> As Little Quack swam without a care.

"Oh, I must see my groom and tailor too,
So I won't be having a swim today.
Then I'll iron my tie and polish one shoe!
So please, Little Quack, dash along with me
While I stay as dapper as a duck can be!"

Catpencil Lid

Consider the case
Of Catpencil Lid,
Because storing pencils
Wasn't all that she did.

She liked holding black pens
And red ones and blue.
She smiled when she used
Her pencil sharpener too.

She knew how to sketch
And she knew how to draw,
With shiny pencils
Held fast in one claw.

She was a utensil
With a whiskery face
And had two cat-paws
That served as a base.

She drew the self-portrait
That you see on this page.
Because with this self-portrait
All her pens could engage!

Harry, the Half-Baked Gingerbread Man

A gingerbread man called Harry
Grew long arms and huge feet.
He tried on a smart new jacket
And Harry looked almost complete.

All Harry needed was shoes,
Then he looked quite a treat
In his freshly baked new shirt
As Harry skipped down the street.

"Hi there, now I'm full-baked!
Would you please just look at me!
And if you like biscuits called 'Harry'
Just invite me over for tea!"

Mr. Caterpillar Aims High

Mr. C is a star,
And he has sixteen legs.
He can kick loads of Sherrins,
Bang! Straight through the pegs.

> He gets plenty of goals,
> Sixteen pots at a shot,
> Dead straight through the middle
> Always bagging the lot!

Fans call him *Cat-thriller*
When he aims at the goals,
As his footies fly high
Going over the poles!

> That pill-kicker's so proud
> When his keen fans all shout,
> His aim's always true,
> As more big ones fly out!

The House on Two Legs

1. The house on two legs
   Went out walking one day,
   He looked for a broom
   And a new silver tray.

2. He looked for a carpet
   And then looked for a mat,
   He looked for a cushion
   And a big tabby cat.

3. He looked for an oven
   Where pancakes could flip,
   Then he looked for a tap
   That would never drip.

4. He knew all his own taps
   They always did that
   As droplets of water
   Fell down and went splat.

5. He puffed from his chimney,
   And he took in the view,
   When he saw other homes
   And their nice gardens too.

6. He walked down the street
   And made friends with a grin,
   So those houses were smiling,
   And especially him.

7. Because taps never leaked here
   On this dry side of town,
   So the house with two legs
   Stopped his drops and sat down!

Fernley, the Little Blast Furnace

This odd walking blast furnace
Little Fernley, he's so proud
He knows how to melt all sorts of ore
And make smoke rise into clouds.

He always belched and burped,
With so much soot and steam,
He could never see just where he was,
But only where he'd been.

He left soot all over earth,
And smoke up in the air,
He covered fields with drifting ash
And threw cinders everywhere.

But that Fernley had a dream,
A dream meant to enchant,
That one day he would be rebuilt
As a nice clean solar plant!

Acknowledgements:

Previously published:

Witches Have Hitches, **Australian Poems for Children**; eds. Clare Scott-Maxwell and Kathlyn Griffith; Illustrated by Gregory Rogers; Random House Australia, 2002.

Party Piece, **A Very First Poetry Book**; Compiled by John Foster; Illustrated by Jan Lewis, Inga Moore and Joe Wright; Oxford University Press; 1984.

The Wilderong, Witches Have Hitches, **The Moving Skull and Other Awesome Australian Verse**; Collected by Michael Dugan; Illustrated by Bruce Riddell; Hodder and Stoughton, 1981.

Double Header, Juniper Jim and *Party Piece,* **More Stuff and Nonsense**; Compiled by Michael Dugan; Illustrated by Roland Harvey; Collins, Sydney, 1980.

The Long-Nosed Smelter, The Wilderong, **Stuff and Nonsense**; Compiled by Michael Dugan; Illustrated by Deborah Niland; William Collins, Sydney, 1974, 1975, 1977, 1982.

* Remaining poems and original drawing by John Jenkins, all previously unpublished.

Note on the Author/Illustrator:

John Jenkins is a widely published poet, short fiction writer and non-fiction writer/editor. He wrote and illustrated most of these poems in 2020, as a positive statement of optimism during the 'corona-virus' lockdown in Australia. He lives on the semi-rural fringe of Melbourne, near the Yarra Valley. More: www.johnjenkins.com.au

Thank you:

To my partner, Shan Shnookal, for her excellent feedback and many helpful suggestions.

www.ingramcontent.com/pod-product-compliance
Lightning Source LLC
Chambersburg PA
CBHW021447080526
44588CB00009B/730